A Word Wreath

CHRISTMAS REFLECTIONS

Marsha MacLeod

WESTBOW
PRESS®
A DIVISION OF THOMAS NELSON
& ZONDERVAN

Scripture taken from the New King James Version®. Copyright © 1982 by Thomas Nelson, Inc. Used by permission. All rights reserved.

WestBow Press books may be ordered through booksellers or by contacting:

WestBow Press
A Division of Thomas Nelson & Zondervan
1663 Liberty Drive
Bloomington, IN 47403
www.westbowpress.com
844-714-3454

ISBN: 978-1-4497-9947-2 (sc)
ISBN: 978-1-4497-9946-5 (e)

Print information available on the last page.

WestBow Press rev. date: 07/21/2021

Revised 2021

Contents

Suggestions for Creating Christmas Poems

Preface

"Swing your eyes upwards in Christmas night.
The stars suggest a celebration."
—Marsha MacLeod

When I began to follow Jesus, I wanted to share my love for God in a Christmas card for my grandfather, an artist who had said that he could no longer draw or paint. Folding a piece of plain paper, I thought about the stars revealing God's power and character. I wrote the words above and mailed the card to my grandfather. As the days passed, he did not acknowledge that he had received the card, and I wondered why. Later an envelope from him came in the mail. Inside, I discovered a card with his drawing of a star-strewn sky illustrating the words I had written—a Christmas card from a grandfather to his granddaughter. I understood more fully then that the Lord can bless our words so that they become a gift of love.

This collection of poems contains suggestions for creating a Word wreath with a child during Advent as well as creating various types of Christmas poems. May you find joy in sharing with others your own reflections about the Lord Jesus and the wonder of His coming.

A Word Wreath

Creating a Word Wreath
with a Child

The seven poems in this section focus on characters in the Christmas story: Joseph, Mary, the shepherds, Simeon, Anna, Herod, and the wise men. With a child, read daily one of the given Bible passages along with the accompanying poem.

Ask the child to choose and write a word or phrase from the Bible passage on a small piece of paper, perhaps using colors or adding a design. Encourage the child to share his or her reason for the selection and to attach the paper to a wreath.

When the week's readings and selection of words are completed, the child will have created a wreath presenting words from God's Word—a Word wreath.

Joseph (Matthew 1:18–25)

To
Joseph
in
a
dream
came
an
angel
sharing
that
he
would
be
the
father
caring
for
Jesus,
the
Son
of
God,
Immanuel,
who
would
save
His
people
from
their
sins
as
Isaiah
did
foretell.

Mary (Luke 1:26–56 and Luke 2:1–7)

In
her
heart
Mary
treasured
angels
singing
"Glory"
in
the
sky
and
shepherds
rejoicing
in
God's
Son,
and
she
delighted
in
the
precious
Child
as
her
spirit
sang
pure
joy
to
the
Holy
One.

Shepherds (Luke 2:8–20)

Shepherds
watching
their
flocks
that
night
had
no
expectation
of
angels
singing
with
adoration
that
in
David's
town
would
be
found
the
One
in
whom
all
peace
abounds.

Simeon (Luke 2:21-35)

The
Holy
Spirit
led
Simeon
to
the
temple
courts
at
Jesus'
consecration,
and
there
Simeon
found
Israel's
consolation
and
light
for
the
Gentiles'
revelation
as
he
held
glory
in
his
arms.

Anna

(Luke 2:36–38)

Anna
learned
to
fast
and
pray,
dwelling
in
the
temple
night
and
day,
and
she
thanked
God
when
she
came
upon
His
Son
and
spoke
to
others
about
the
coming
of
the
Promised
One.

Herod

(Matthew 2:1-23)

Herod
should
have
seen,
for
no
star
had
appeared
when
he
was
born,
that
the
king
the
wise
men
sought
was
God
in
flesh
made
known,

whom
one
does
not
approach
by
sending
soldiers
with
hearts
of
stone
to
murder
baby
boys.

Magi

(Matthew 2:9-12)

Magi,
who
came
to
find
the
one
for
whom
a
bright
star
shone,
bowed
down
and
worshiped
the
King
of
kings,

who
had
left
his
throne—
Jesus,
the
Bright
Morning
Star
who
would
claim
us
as
His
own.

Poems about Jesus

"In the beginning was the Word, and the Word was with God, and the Word was God" (John 1:1).

"Let this mind be in you which was also in Christ Jesus, who, being in the form of God, did not consider it robbery to be equal with God, but made Himself of no reputation, taking the form of a bondservant, and coming in the likeness of men" (Philippians 2:5–7).

His Love, His Light, His Life

Love with Love dwelling,
wonder compelling,
worshiping angels behold and adore.
Wisdom all knowing,
holy wind blowing,
coming the time long determined before.

Light with Light shining,
Mercy inclining,
silently exiles searching the darkness.
Sovereignty viewing,
Goodness pursuing,
Faithfulness raising shimmering promise.

Life with Life giving,
Truth ever living,
bright glory blazing near Justice's face.
With the Son leaving,
our world receiving
God's gift:
a baby on us breathing Grace.

"And she will bring forth a Son, and you shall call His name JESUS, for He will save His people from their sins" *(Matthew 1:21).*

Salvation

Salvation
lying
in
a
manger,
once
wrapped
in
light,
now
wrapped
in
flesh,
a
stranger
to
sin

yet
approachable
here,
and
for
love
of
us
so
dependent,
this
Son
from
unapproachable
light
resplendent.

"For unto us a Child is born,
Unto us a Son is given;
And the government will be upon His shoulder.
And His name will be called
Wonderful, Counselor, Mighty God,
Everlasting Father, Prince of Peace" (Isaiah 9:6).

The Promised One

Promises,
which
God
had
spoken,
foretold
the
coming
of
the
Son,
and
God,
faithful
to
His
Word,
in
Yeshua
fulfilled
each
one.

Jesus

A sure promise: victory, not shame,   Genesis 3:15
The Lord's blessings flowing down through time, Genesis 12:3
Forever a royal throne bearing David's name,   2 Samuel 7:16
The scepter to stay in Judah until Messiah came.   Genesis 49:10

Then, by virgin born, the Lord's own sign,   Isaiah 7:14
Sent to "prepare the way," His messenger bold,   Malachi 3:1
"Unto us a Son is given"—a Son divine,   Isaiah 9:6–7
On those in darkness "a light has shined."   Isaiah 9:1–2

Out of Bethlehem, One "from of old,"   Micah 5:2
The hope of rejoicing hearts: Immanuel,   Isaiah 7:14
One like Moses—a great prophet as foretold,   Deuteronomy 18:15
Rachel mourning children   Jeremiah 31:15
     she would no longer hold.

Called out of Egypt, where He did dwell,   Hosea 11:1
The Anointed One, whom God would reveal,   Isaiah 61:1–6
Hear the voices of children praising Him well,   Psalm 8:2
"THE LORD OUR RIGHTEOUSNESS"   Jeremiah 23:5–6
     the prophet did foretell.

Lowly the King whom we would adore,   Zechariah 9:9

"Acquainted with grief" and our iniquity, Isaiah 53:3–6

A friend who was trusted—a conspirator, Psalm 41:9

The chief cornerstone to be the stone   Psalm 118:22-23
  rejected before.

The Shepherd stricken, the sheep will flee, Zechariah 13:7

A princely sum thrown in the house   Zechariah 11:12-13
  of the Lord,

Struck and spat upon: both shame and agony, Isaiah 50:6

Amid sinners He would bear our sins upon a tree. Isaiah 53:12

Trust in the heavenly Father, whom He knew, Psalm 31:5

Not a single bone broken—none,   Psalm 34:20

"But with the rich at His death"—   Isaiah 53:9
  God's Word ever true,

The safekeeping of His own, as only God can do. Psalm 16:10–11

Behold: The King of Glory, the Son,   Psalm 24:7–10

The Lord now sitting at the Lord's right hand, Psalm 110:1

Messiah, Priest Forever, and Holy One, Psalm 110:4

Promised Scepter through whom our victory Numbers 24:17
  has been won!

"He was in the world, and the world was made through Him, and the world did not know Him. He came to His own, and His own did not receive Him. But as many as received Him, to them He gave the right to become children of God, to those who believe in His name: who were born, not of blood, nor of the will of the flesh, nor of the will of man, but of God" (John 1:10–13).

His Birth

The night felt the fire of a star.
On those in the dark the Light shone.
All men had wandered afar.
The Son of Man came to His own.

The wise men followed, star blazing.
The Wisdom of God was on earth.
Shepherds heard angels praising.
A Savior born at the Lamb's birth.

"The people who walked in darkness
Have seen a great light;
Those who dwelt in the land of the shadow of death,
Upon them a light has shined" (Isaiah 9:2).

Glorious Light

A pillar of fire
burned
through the night
for those
in the wilderness.
They found
God will guide,
protect, provide.
In the dark
His Presence
is light.

A baby
is sleeping
now tonight.
"Glory!" resounds
through the skies.
Behold, God the Son,
the Holy One—
in the dark
our glorious
Light.

Yes, God the Son,
the Holy One—
in the dark
our glorious
Light.

"Then the angel said to them, 'Do not be afraid, for behold, I bring you good tidings of great joy which will be to all people. For there is born to you this day in the city of David a Savior, who is Christ the Lord'" (Luke 2:10–11).

Eyes of Faith

Eyes
of
faith
gaze
upon
the
Savior
in
a
manger
as
"Glory!"
echoes
in
hearts
and
minds,
and
as
the
baby
stirs
in
slumber,
souls
awake
to
newborn
wonder.

"Now when they had seen Him, they made widely known the saying which was told them concerning this Child. And all those who heard it marveled at those things which were told them by the shepherds" (Luke 2:17–18).

In the Fields at Night

Shepherds watching in the fields at night
were surrounded by glory shining bright.
An angel told them good news of great joy:

Born to you in David's town a baby boy,
"a Savior, who is Christ the Lord."

Others watch now in the fields at night.
May they see in us the Lord's shining light.
May they hear from us good news of great joy:

Born to you in David's town a baby boy,
"a Savior, who is Christ the Lord."

"And Jesus said to them, 'I am the bread of life. He who comes to Me shall never hunger, and he who believes in Me shall never thirst'" (John 6:35).

The Bread of Life

In
Bethlehem
an
offering
come
down
from
heaven
to
satisfy
the
hunger
of
the
soul,

and
for
love
of
us
in
the
fullness
of
time
the
Bread
of
Life
broken
so
we
can
be
whole.

"For indeed Christ, our Passover, was sacrificed for us"
(1 Corinthians 5:7).

Breathtaking Nativity

"Glory to God
in the highest"
crescendos
through
the
skies
while
in
Bethlehem
the
heart
of
God's Son
beats
quietly
to
the
rhythm
of
"I AM."

Breathtaking
nativity
for
the
Son
of
God
would
be
our
Passover
Lamb.

"Now after Jesus was born in Bethlehem of Judea in the days of Herod the king, behold, wise men from the East came to Jerusalem, saying, 'Where is He who has been born King of the Jews? For we have seen His star in the East and have come to worship Him.'

"When Herod the king heard this, he was troubled, and all Jerusalem with him" (Matthew 2:1–3).

In the Father's Safekeeping

Troubling—
> this news of a star and king
> that darkness in the city
> is whispering.

Joyous—
> the worship of God's Son
> when knowing
> what the Almighty has done.

Warning—
> the angel's words in a dream
> of a vengeful king
> and his murderous scheme.

Faithful—
        two trusting at night
        in the Father's safekeeping
        their family in flight.

Exiles—
        in Egypt rising at last
        with the threat of devouring sword
        having passed.

Sanctuary—
        in Nazareth found
        for the One who for us
        would lay His life down.

"When they saw the star, they rejoiced with exceedingly great joy. And when they had come into the house, they saw the young Child with Mary His mother, and fell down and worshiped Him. And when they had opened their treasures, they presented gifts to Him: gold, frankincense, and myrrh" (Matthew 2:10–11).

Living Treasure

Worshiping, they bowed down to Jesus,
offering gold, frankincense, and myrrh.
They had journeyed through night,
following starlight,
and found living treasure.

Worshiping, we bow down to Jesus,
offering ourselves to the Savior.
May we journey through night,
following His light,
and share heart-held treasure.

"And Jesus came and spoke to them, saying, 'All authority has been given to Me in heaven and on earth. Go therefore and make disciples of all the nations, baptizing them in the name of the Father and of the Son and of the Holy Spirit, teaching them to observe all things that I have commanded you; and lo, I am with you always, even to the end of the age.' Amen" (Matthew 28:18–20).

Worship in the Gospel of Matthew

Falling down, wise men worshiped
the King, heralded by a star,
great joy infusing
these men choosing
heaven's treasure from afar.

Boldly a leper worshiped,
proclaiming faith in God the Son,
and heard Love's thrilling
"I am willing"
with the touch of the Holy One.

Humbly a ruler worshiped,
asking God to raise his daughter,
soon realizing
her arising,
for seeing his faith, Love sought her.

With reverence, disciples worshiped,
having found in a boat at sea
amidst winds blowing
a new knowing
of wondrous Love's identity.

Persistently a mother worshiped,
though her child in demonic possession,
to God appealing,
her faith revealing,
and Love answered her profession.

Joyfully women worshiped
when Jesus met them and they drew near,
at His feet falling,
Love enthralling,
there finding, yes, love casts out fear.

Expectantly may we worship,
responsive to Love's persuasions,
a new song singing,
our gifts bringing,
as we go to all the nations.

"But the angel answered and said to the women, 'Do not be afraid, for I know that you seek Jesus who was crucified. He is not here; for He is risen, as He said. Come, see the place where the Lord lay'" (Matthew 28:5–6).

Words of Resurrection

A stone rolled away
speaks, "Mystery,"
when an earthquake
rumbles, "Death."

A folded cloth
whispers, "Eternity,"
as a garden
holds its breath.

An angel proclaims,
"He is risen."
Hope rises and cries,
"Can it be?"

Then, as Jesus appears
to a woman in tears
and speaks her name,
the empty tomb
shouts, "Victory!"

*"And every creature which is in heaven and on the earth
and under the earth and such as are in the sea, and all that
are in them, I heard saying:*

'Blessing and honor and glory and power
Be to Him who sits on the throne,
And to the Lamb, forever and ever!'" (Revelation 5:13)

Praise Forever

Light,
phenomenal,
in the darkness
proclaiming a King
invincible.

The way,
sacrificial,
the cross an altar,
with God's holy blood
essential.

Love,
triumphal,
risen from the grave,
offering hope and life
eternal.

Praise
irrepressible:
in Jesus,
God's goodness
forever expressible.

"But He was wounded for our transgressions,
He was bruised for our iniquities;
The chastisement for our peace was upon Him,
And by His stripes we are healed" (Isaiah 53:5).

His Hands

So small the hands
of the Son of God,
veiled miracle
this newborn's hold:
God Himself,
through whom
all things were made,
here making baby hands unfold.

Vigorous the clasp
of the Carpenter,
familiar with man
and with wood:
God,
whose thoughts
outnumber the sand,
His kingdom at first misunderstood.

Compassionate the touch
of the Physician
on the hurting
and the outcast:
God,
despised
and rejected by men,
His mercy remaining steadfast.

Obedient the reach
of the Servant,
His cup
from the Father above:
God,
enduring my sin
on the cross,
distinctive sign language of love.

Nail scarred, the hands
of our risen Savior,
and surrounding me
I now find
a shield of love
from my Lord and my God,
to whom I hand
heart, soul, and mind.

"And suddenly there was with the angel a multitude of the heavenly host praising God and saying:

'Glory to God in the highest,
And on earth peace, goodwill toward men!'"
(Luke 2:13-14)

Discernible

Beloved Son
leaving
heaven's
glory
to
dwell
among
us—
human divinity.

Savior
lying
in
a
manger
amidst
dusty
travelers—
profound simplicity.

Lamb of God
enduring
the
cross
for
love
of
us—
discernible mystery.

Jesus:
His
peace
healing
and
shielding
hearts
and
minds
almightily—
the Gift the Giver.

"And the Word became flesh and dwelt among us, and we beheld His glory, the glory as of the only begotten of the Father, full of grace and truth" (John 1:14).

Branches and Vine

Branches and Vine,
water to wine,
the Word our hearts revealing.
Darkness and light,
blindness to sight,
God's flow of power healing.

Pride and humbleness,
discord to oneness,
God's Son as Servant appealing.
Trespass and grace,
fear to peace,
our hearts His heart feeling.

Cross and desolation,
death and Resurrection,
despair finds joy enfolding.
Lost now found,
manger to crown,
we His glory beholding.

"So it was, when the angels had gone away from them into heaven, that the shepherds said to one another, 'Let us now go to Bethlehem and see this thing that has come to pass, which the Lord has made known to us'" (Luke 2:15).

Where Are We Going?

Shepherds followed the words of an angel.
Wise men followed a beckoning star.
Earth was startled by a newborn's cry
and "Glory!" resounding in the sky.

Where are we going?
Whom do we follow?
What should we carry?
How should we go?

Those who follow the footsteps of Jesus
will follow the road to Calvary,
where earth once heard a triumphant cry
rise from a cross through a darkened sky.

Where are we going?
Whom do we follow?
What should we carry?
How should we go?

The Son of God still calls to us clearly
to take up our cross and follow Him,
yet coming the day when earth shall cry
as Christ comes with glory in the sky.

Homeward we're going.
Jesus we follow.
A cross we carry.
Love shows us how.

"Therefore, brethren, having boldness to enter the Holiest by the blood of Jesus, by a new and living way which He consecrated for us, through the veil, that is, His flesh, and having a High Priest over the house of God, let us draw near with a true heart in full assurance of faith, having our hearts sprinkled from an evil conscience and our bodies washed with pure water" (Hebrews 10:19–22).

"Jesus said to him, 'I am the way, the truth, and the life. No one comes to the Father except through Me'" (John 14:6).

The Way, the Truth, and the Life

The Way
new
and
living
with
God
giving
entry
into
His
Presence
on
the
journey.

The Truth
illuminating
with
the
Word
resonating
in
hearts
and
minds
of
travelers
who
know
that
they
are
free.

The Life
recreating
with
God's
love
forever
captivating
sons
and
daughters
of
Majesty.

"Then the shepherds returned, glorifying and praising God for all the things they had heard and seen, as it was told them" (Luke 2:20).

When We Know

When we know
He is Lord,
the darkest
of nights
can become
Spirit bright
as we worship
like shepherds
and angels
of the skies,
seeing the Savior
with truth-lit eyes.

"Let this mind be in you which was also in Christ Jesus, who, being in the form of God, did not consider it robbery to be equal with God, but made Himself of no reputation, taking the form of a bondservant and coming in the likeness of men" (Philippians 2:5-7)

With His Coming

With His "coming
in the likeness of men,"
came God's glory
illuminating night,
and angels announcing
the Savior's birth
to shepherds surrounded
by shining light.

With His coming again,
Jesus will come
with clouds and angels
and wondrous glory,
quelling opposition
and compelling recognition
that He is the Son of God--
the Savior and the world's Light.

"And the Word became flesh and dwelt among us, and we beheld His glory, the glory as of the only begotten of the Father, full of grace and truth" (John 1:14).

God's Glory

An angel proclaims
the Savior's birth,
glory surrounds
shepherds in a field,
and under a night-time sky
a multitude of angels
praise God on high.

Amidst
a wedding celebration
with wine
no longer flowing,
Jesus turns water
into wine,
and his disciples then,
beholding glory,
believe in him.

Praying on a mountain,
Jesus is transfigured,
his face shines radiantly,
and as he speaks
with Moses and Elijah,
slumbering disciples
awake to glory.

Jesus weeps
when his friend
Lazarus dies,
but he foresees
God's glory.
Standing at the tomb,
in a loud voice
Jesus cries,
"Lazarus, come forth!"

And hearing
the Son of God
call his name,
Lazarus came.

"But Mary stood outside by the tomb weeping, and as she wept she stooped down and looked into the tomb. And she saw two angels in white sitting, one at the head and the other at the feet, where the body of Jesus had lain. Then they said to her, "Woman, why are you weeping?" (John 20:11-13).

Angels

An angel explaining to a blessed virgin
that her firstborn Son forever will be
the reigning King of kings

An angel sharing with a man dreaming
that the man is to be the earthly father
caring for the Son of God

Angels announcing to shepherds,
watching their flocks at night,
that in David's town will be found
"a Savior, who is Christ the Lord"

Jesus contending with the words
of the tempter in the wilderness,
and afterwards angels attending
to the Word made flesh

An angel appearing in a garden,
strengthening the Son,
who had been praying to His Father,
"not My will, but Yours, be done"

Two angels sitting in an empty tomb,
and Mary Magdalene nearby weeping,
but then Jesus speaks her name,
and the inconceivable becomes believable.

"When the Son of Man comes in His glory, and all the holy angels with Him, then He will sit on the throne of His glory" (Matthew 25:31)

Suddenly

Suddenly
at night
on earth
shining glory
and an angel
announcing
the Savior's
birth.
Together
angels
praise God,
and shepherds
journey to see
humbly born
royalty.

Suddenly
on the clouds
of heaven
the Son of Man
coming
in His glory,
"and all
the holy angels
with Him."
All the earth
one day to see
the King's
resplendent
majesty.

"Now faith is the substance of things hoped for, the evidence of things not seen" (Hebrews 11:1).

Faith Can

Faith can go where God is sending,
destination unknown,
for faith knows that we are pilgrims
on a journey for home.

Faith can climb high mountain places,
walk the ridges windblown,
trusting Jesus who has promised
we will not walk alone.

"Beloved, now we are children of God; and it has not yet been revealed what we shall be, but we know that when He is revealed, we shall be like Him, for we shall see Him as He is" (1 John 3:2).

Immanuel Now Waiting

Immanuel now waiting,
hope on earth permeating,
through Him, life with Him obtained.

God's love so surprising,
thankfulness rising,
earthen vessels await final change.

At last, Death's sting removing,
Resurrection proving,
beloved Son forever to reign.

Though once eyes of faith seeing,
finally we like Him being,
Oh, Love's persevering campaign.

Suggestions for Creating Christmas Poems

Acrostic Poems

The simplest kind of acrostic poem adds a word, group of words, or sentence after the letters in the word that frames the poem. In the example below, each of the letters in the word *STAR* presents a phrase describing the bright star that the wise men followed.

S hining so brightly
T raveling across the sky
A nnouncing the coming of a King
R esting above the house where the Child lay

More complex acrostic poems exist, such as those that form a complete sentence as a person reads through the words. The following acrostic poem associates the wise men's gift of gold with God's gift of His Son:

G od
O ffers
L ove
D ivine

All kinds of acrostic poems have yet to be written. In particular, the many names of Jesus provide opportunities to meditate on who He is and communicate His identity to others.

Choose the word *Lord* or another word to create an acrostic poem.

_____

_____

_____

Concrete Poems

A concrete poem—a shaped poem—produces a visual image related to its words. One of the early writers of concrete poems, George Herbert, arranged lines to form the image of a stone altar as he compared his heart to an altar. In "Easter Wings," Herbert shaped his lines into outspread wings and declared that he could rise and soar with Christ because of Christ's Resurrection and victory over sin.

Later poets experimented with basic and complex images. Sometimes they broke apart words or lines to create images related to Christmas. Emily Huntington Miller's "Hang Up the Baby's Stocking!" conveys love for a baby sister celebrating her first Christmas. The speaker in the poem notices the baby's tiny toes and realizes that her tiny Christmas stocking will not hold much at all. Therefore, the speaker concludes that one of Grandma's long stockings must be substituted so that the baby's stocking can be stuffed with gifts. Lines are broken in the middle of sentences to create the shape of an exceptionally long stocking.

Basic shapes—a star, a shepherd's staff, the cross, or a crown—can become Christmas poems. You may want to use a shape that will represent a favorite Christmas memory. Feel free to use single words, groups of words, or sentences in your poem. If you have much to say, arrange the words to form and fill a shape. However, if you plan to use few words, create a simple outline of the shape with the words.

A Concrete Poem

List Poems

List poems often are free-verse poems—poems that usually do not conform to fixed patterns of rhyme or rhythm. A line may consist of a sentence, group of words, or single word because the poet creates a framework unique for the specific poem.

One type of list poem presents questions. For example, the Bible tells us that the shepherds told others what they had seen on the night that the Savior was born. What might have been some questions that people asked when they heard what the shepherds had seen and heard? What question or questions would you have asked the shepherds?

List possible questions.

_____

_____

_____

_____

_____

_____

_____

_____

_____

Now arrange the questions and any answers that you would like to include in a free-verse poem. Look for ways to create variety in your arrangement with contrasting ideas, distinctive language, and perhaps unexpected line lengths. If you are not sure how to begin, come back to the introduction after you have written the body of the poem. Remember that poems can begin in the middle of a thought or an action.

You may decide to emphasize the importance of an idea by repeating words or to arrange a sentence so that its words flow from one line to the next. Consider checking a thesaurus if word options are needed. Perhaps conclude with an observation of your own.

A List Poem

_____

_____

_____

_____

_____

_____

_____

_____

_____

Images and the Senses

We form images with impressions gathered by our five senses: sight, sound, taste, smell, and touch. Close your eyes and imagine what you, as a traveler arriving in Bethlehem, might have noticed on the night that Jesus was born. Can you describe what you might have seen, heard, tasted, smelled, and touched?

Sight: _____

_____

_____

_____

Sound: _____

_____

_____

_____

Taste: _____

_____

_____

_____

Smell: _____

_____

_____

_____

Touch: _____

_____

_____

_____

Personification

Personification is a description of a thing or an idea as if it were a person or an animal. For example, "I Heard the Bells on Christmas Day" characterizes bells as speaking: "Then pealed the bells more loud and deep: 'God is not dead, nor doth He sleep.'"

Hebrew poetry in the Old Testament occasionally uses personification. The book of Proverbs personifies wisdom as a woman.

> Does not wisdom cry out,
> And understanding lift up her voice?
> She takes her stand on the top of the high hill,
> Beside the way, where the paths meet.
> —Proverbs 8:1-2

At the time of Jesus' birth, people in Israel continued to hope for the promised Messiah—God's anointed king who would deliver them from their enemies and establish a new kingdom. Describe the thoughts, words, or actions of Hope as a person in crowded Bethlehem when Jesus was born. Include some of the sensory experiences—sight, sound, taste, smell, or touch—that you listed previously for a traveler in Bethlehem.

Personification of Hope

_____

_____

_____

_____

Similes and Metaphors

Similes and metaphors are images that compare two basically different things. A simile uses *like* or *as*. For example, the psalmist in Psalm 119:176 compares himself to a sheep by saying, "I have gone astray like a lost sheep." On the other hand, a metaphor does not use *like* or *as* and implies that two different things are the same in at least one way. David begins Psalm 23:1 by declaring, "The LORD is my shepherd," and then develops the comparison.

Can you complete the following similes and metaphors from the psalms?

"The words of the LORD are pure words,
Like _____ tried in a furnace of earth,
Purified seven times" (Psalm 12:6).

"You are my _____;
You shall preserve me from trouble;
You shall surround me with songs of deliverance"
(Psalm 32:7).

"Your righteousness is like the great _____"
(Psalm 36:6).

"As the _____ pants for the water brooks,
So pants my soul for You, O God" (Psalm 42:1).

"My heart is overflowing with a good theme;
I recite my composition concerning the King;
My tongue is the _____ of a ready writer" (Psalm 45:1).

"His words were softer than oil,
Yet they were _____" (Psalm 55:21).

"Your word is a _____ to my feet
And a light to my path" (Psalm 119:105).

Christmas carols contain some beautiful similes and metaphors. "Lo, How a Rose E'er Blooming," a Christmas carol probably written in the Middle Ages, creates a well-developed metaphor that compares Jesus to a rose "whose fragrance tender / With sweetness fills the air." In "Silent Night," Joseph Mohr describes the birth of Jesus metaphorically as "the dawn of redeeming grace."

Remembering what the Bible tells us in the gospels of Matthew and Luke about the shepherds and wise men, complete the sentences below with your descriptive similes and metaphors.

1. Simile: The shepherds were "greatly afraid" like _____

_____

2. Metaphor: The words of the angel of the Lord were ____

_____

3. Simile: The shepherds hastened to the manger like ____

_____

4. Metaphor: The star was _____

_____

5. Simile: Herod was angry like _____

_____

6. Metaphor: The joy of the wise men was _____

_____

Persona Poems

When a poet writes in the voice of an identifiable character, the poet creates a persona poem. Christmas persona poems have been written from the viewpoint of an array of characters, such as Joseph, Mary, an innkeeper, a shepherd boy, and even animals in the manger.

After the poet T. S. Eliot decided to follow Jesus, he wrote a persona poem in which one of the wise men reflects on the birth of Christ. Before creating your own persona poem about one of the wise men, review what the Bible tells us and think about the following questions:

1. What would have been the challenges of following a bright star at night?
2. What might have seemed unusual to the wise men when they arrived in Jerusalem?
3. How did God provide what they needed?
4. How did their journey end?

A Persona Poem

_____

_____

_____

_____

_____

_____

Rhymes

In previous centuries, musicians and poets performed their ballads, songs, and poems for audiences who listened for rhyme and the repetition of sounds. As a result, songwriters and poets experimented with the repetition of vowels and consonants as well as with rhyme.

Songwriters and poets rhymed words at the end of consecutive or alternating lines. Sometimes the repetition of the same word solved the need for a rhyme. Intricate rhyme patterns developed, and internal rhyme appeared within lines. Writers produced approximate or slant rhyme with words that sounded somewhat similar, such as *Lord* and *Word.*

Without referring to a rhyming dictionary, think of a few meaningful words that rhyme with the following words:

Night   _____

Glory   _____

Love   _____

Peace   _____

Praise   _____

Star   _____

Immanuel   _____

King   _____

Joy   _____

Son   _____

Alliteration and Consonance

Alliteration and consonance can create a delightful sequence of sounds. Alliteration is the repetition of identical consonant sounds usually at the beginning of words near each other. Consonance is the repetition of identical consonant sounds usually in the middle or the end of words nearby.

Underline repeated consonant sounds in the following carols:

"The world in solemn stillness lay
To hear the angels sing."
 —"It Came Upon the Midnight Clear," by Edmund H. Sears

"Disperse the gloomy clouds of night,
And death's dark shadows put to flight."
—"O Come, O Come, Emmanuel," a hymn from the Middle Ages

"Field and fountain, moor and mountain,
Following yonder star."
 —"We Three Kings of Orient Are," by John H. Hopkins Jr.

Create a sentence about Christmas with words that have an "s" sound.

_____

_____

Create a sentence about Christmas with words that repeat another consonant sound.

_____

_____

Assonance

Assonance—the repetition of vowel sounds in words near one another—enhances the appeal of song lyrics or poems. Songwriters know that some vowel sounds are especially easy to sing and are pleasant sounding.

Underline repeated vowel sounds in the following carols:

"O, holy night, the stars are brightly shining."
  —"O Holy Night," English words by John Sullivan Dwight

"Rejoice! Rejoice! Emmanuel
Shall come to thee, O Israel!"
  —"O Come, O Come, Emmanuel," a hymn from the Middle Ages

Create a sentence about Christmas with words that have a long "o" sound.

_____

_____

_____

Create a sentence about Christmas with words that have a long "i" sound.

_____

_____

_____

Rhythm in Words

Christmas carols contain memorable names for Jesus. Stressed and unstressed syllables in the words can easily be identified by capitalizing each stressed syllable: JE-sus. If a name has one syllable, the syllable is considered stressed: LORD. In a word with several syllables, such as *Em-man-u-el,* there may be two stressed syllables—one with more stress ("man") and one with less stress ("el"): em-MAN-u-EL.

Write the following names for Jesus, capitalizing the stressed syllables:

Mes-si-ah _____

Day-spring _____

When words combine into a phrase or sentence, patterns with stressed and unstressed syllables can develop. Some types of words are usually unstressed when spoken: *a, an, the, and, or, to, with, of, on, am, is, are, was,* and *were.* For instance, "the Son of God" has a pattern of alternating unstressed and stressed syllables: the SON of GOD.

People sometimes can hear different rhythms. The lyrics in "Silent Night" refer to Jesus as "love's pure light." A person could hear the words as "LOVE'S pure LIGHT" or "LOVE'S pure light."

Write the following name that Jesus used to describe Himself, capitalizing the stressed syllables according to the rhythm that you hear:

The Re-sur-rec-tion and the Life

_____

Song Lyrics

Contemporary writers of poems and song lyrics often use the natural rhythms of everyday speech. Some writers develop a combination of rhythms while others do not focus on arranging words rhythmically. When writing a phrase or sentence, keep in mind that each word has a rhythm-making possibility.

Infinite rhythmic patterns can occur within songs when a writer combines musical rhythms with rhythms in the words. Songwriters frequently create a combination of patterns to provide variety.

Tap the simple rhythmic patterns in the words below, tapping stressed syllables with more emphasis than unstressed syllables:

Unstressed-Stressed Pattern of Syllables:

"i HEARD the BELLS on CHRIST-mas DAY."
—"I Heard the Bells on Christmas Day," words by
Henry W. Longfellow

Stressed-Unstressed Pattern of Syllables:

"BORN to RAISE the SONS of EARTH,
BORN to GIVE them SEC-ond BIRTH."
—"Hark! The Herald Angels Sing,"
original words by Charles Wesley

In the following carols, syllables are indicated but not identified as stressed or unstressed. Tap the diverse word rhythms that you hear.

"No-el, No-el, No-el, No-el,
Born is the King of Is-ra-el."
—"The First Noel," a traditional carol

"Go tell it on the moun-tain,
O-ver the hills and ev'-ry-where."
—"Go Tell It on the Mountain," a traditional spiritual

In earlier centuries, people found it natural to create additional verses for existing folk carols. They occasionally created songs by composing new lyrics for familiar tunes. Copyright law did not exist. "What Child Is This?" began as a poem by William Dix that someone later combined with the well-known music of "Greensleeves."

Inspiration for a song can occur in vastly different circumstances. As Christmas Eve approached in 1818, Joseph Mohr, a priest in an Austrian village, discovered that the church's organ was broken. He hurried to the organist, Franz Gruber, with a poem he had written and asked if Franz could set the words to music with guitar chords. That evening the poem "Silent Night" was sung in church for the first time. In the United States during the Civil War, Henry Wadsworth Longfellow was inspired to write the poem "I Heard the Bells on Christmas Day" in the midst of the widespread suffering. Years later in England, J.B. Calkin set the words to music.

As you reflect on the meaning of Christmas, think of an idea for a song and then write a simple song or chorus that you or someone else could set to music.

Christmas Lyrics

_____

_____

_____

_____

_____

_____

Prayer Poems and Prayer Songs

Jesus tells us in John 8:12, "I am the light of the world." Think about the times that you have been thankful for physical and spiritual light. Perhaps you remember venturing outdoors on a moonless night with a flashlight or knowing God's light and guidance from His Word when facing a difficult decision. Jot down memories, and look up some of the references to light in the Bible. Ask God for his help in writing a prayer poem or song about light and about Jesus—the Light of the World.

We have a wonderful legacy of written prayers, prayer poems, and prayer songs from known and unknown writers. If you want to share with others your prayer poem or song, place the words out of sight for a while. Reading the words aloud later on, you may notice additional ways to unite the ideas, images, rhythms, and sounds.

A Prayer Poem or Prayer Song

_____

_____

_____

_____

_____

_____

_____

_____

Do you have an idea for designing a Christmas card with an acrostic or a concrete poem for friends? Would you enjoy reading a persona poem to your family? Perhaps you would like to write and record a prayer poem or song.

Whatever you do, look for a way to share your words. Words about Jesus can be a wonderful gift.

Printed in the United States
by Baker & Taylor Publisher Services